TEENAGERS

TEACHING CHILDREN

A 4-week course to help teenagers
teach the basics of their faith

by Jennifer Root Wilger

Group®

Loveland, Colorado

Group®

Teenagers Teaching Children
Copyright © 1994 Group Publishing, Inc.

First Printing

Credits
Edited by Stephen Parolini
Cover designed by Liz Howe and Amy Bryant

ISBN 1-55945-405-9
Printed in the United States of America

CONTENTS

Teenagers Teaching Children

Lesson 1   9

Planning the Project

Students will study Jesus' teaching style and plan upper-elementary lessons using similar methods.

Lesson 2   20

What Can Kids Learn?

Students will discover the importance of teaching kids the good news.

Lesson 3   25

What Can Kids Teach Us?

Students will explore Jesus' teachings about becoming like children.

Lesson 4   30

Harvesting the Seeds

Students will reflect on their teaching experiences and discover ways to encourage kids to grow in their faith.

Bonus Ideas   35

Introduction

TEENAGERS TEACHING CHILDREN

In the eyes of an 8-year-old, the teenagers in your class are heroes. They get to drive cars and go out on dates—glamorous pursuits that upper-elementary kids can only dream of and look forward to. Your teenagers have a unique window into these kids' lives. Why not bring the gospel message through before the window closes?

Teenagers Teaching Children provides a meaningful way to help your teenagers communicate the gospel message to the next generation. Your teenagers will study Jesus' teaching methods, then use those same methods to teach simple gospel lessons to the upper-elementary students in your church.

Although it may not always seem like they're ready for responsibility, today's teenagers are tomorrow's teachers. The faith development of the next generation lies in their hands. These four lessons will allow your teenagers to experience firsthand the responsibilities and privileges of teaching. And as they develop teaching skills, they'll learn important lessons about themselves, their faith, and the younger generation growing up around them.

Nothing internalizes what we know better than teaching it to others. Use this course to strengthen your teenagers' faith and to help them strengthen the faith of others.

COURSE OBJECTIVES

By the end of this course, your students will
- discover Jesus' teaching methods,
- understand why it's important to pass the gospel message on to a new generation,
- plan and teach three upper-elementary lessons from the Sermon on the Mount,
- learn childlike qualities that are important to God, and
- commit to "water" the "gospel seeds" they've sown by forming a relationship with upper-elementary students.

THIS COURSE AT A GLANCE

Before you dive into the lessons, familiarize yourself with each lesson aim. Then read the Scripture passages.
- Study them as a background to the lessons.
- Use them as a basis for your personal devotions.
- Think about how they relate to kids' circumstances today.

Lesson 1: PLANNING THE PROJECT
Lesson Aim: Students will study Jesus' teaching style and plan upper-elementary lessons using similar methods.
Bible Basis: John 16:12.

Lesson 2: WHAT CAN KIDS LEARN?
Lesson Aim: Students will discover the importance of teaching kids the good news.
Bible Basis: Psalm 78:1-7.

Lesson 3: WHAT CAN KIDS TEACH US?
Lesson Aim: Students will explore Jesus' teachings about becoming like children.
Bible Basis: Matthew 18:1-5 and 1 John 5:1-5.

Lesson 4: HARVESTING THE SEEDS
Lesson Aim: Students will reflect on their teaching experiences and discover ways to encourage kids to grow in their faith.
Bible Basis: Luke 8:4-15.

HOW TO USE THIS COURSE

PROJECTS WITH A PURPOSE™ for Youth Ministry

Think back on an important lesson you've learned in life. Did you learn it by reading about it? from hearing a lecture about it?

Chances are, the most important lessons you've learned came from something you experienced. That's what active learning is—learning by doing. And active learning is a key element in Group's new Projects With a Purpose™ for Youth Ministry courses.

Active learning leads students in doing things that help them understand important principles, messages, and ideas. It's a discovery process that helps kids internalize what they learn.

Research about active learning indicates that maximum learning results when students are involved in direct, purposeful experiences. With that in mind, each Projects With a Purpose for Youth Ministry course gives teachers tools to facilitate some sort of project which results in direct, purposeful experiences for teenagers. Projects, experiences, and immersion into real-life faith action characterize this curriculum. In fact, you could probably call this the "project" curriculum, since each course produces a tangible result. You'll find plenty of helpful hints that'll make this course easy for you to teach and meaningful to your students.

Projects With a Purpose for Youth Ministry takes learning to a new level—giving teenagers an opportunity to discover something significant about their faith. And kids learn the important skills of working together, sharing one another's troubles, and supporting each other in love.

Projects With a Purpose for Youth Ministry offers a fun, alternative way for teenagers to put their faith in action. Use it today to involve your kids in Christian growth experiences they'll remember for a lifetime.

Before the 4-Week Course

■ Read the Introduction, the Course Objectives, and This Course at a Glance.
■ Determine when you'll use this course. Projects With a Purpose for Youth Ministry works well in Sunday school classes, midweek meetings, home Bible studies, youth groups, special interest groups, leadership groups, retreats, camps, or any time you want to help teenagers discover more about their faith.
■ Decide how you'll publicize the course using the clip art on the Publicity Page (p. 8). Prepare fliers, newsletter articles, and posters as needed.
■ Look at the Bonus Ideas (p. 35) and decide which ones you'll use.

Before Each Lesson

Read the opening statements, Objectives, and Bible Basis for the lesson. The Bible Basis focuses on a key biblical theme for the activity, experience, or Bible study portion of the lesson.

Gather necessary supplies from This Lesson at a Glance.

Read each section of the lesson. Adjust where necessary for your class size and meeting room.

Helpful Hints

■ The approximate minutes listed give you an idea of how long each activity will take. Each lesson in a Projects With a Purpose for Youth Ministry course is designed to take about an hour. Some lessons may require work outside of class, depending on the project for the course. You might also consider restructuring your class time, if possible, to allow more time to complete projects.

> The answers given after discussion questions are responses your students *might* give. They aren't the only answers or the "right" answers. If needed, use them to spark discussion. Kids won't always say what you wish they'd say. That's why some of the responses given are negative or controversial. If someone responds negatively, don't be shocked. Accept the person and use the opportunity to explore other angles of the issue.

■ If you see you're going to have extra time, do an activity or two from the "If You Still Have Time..." section at the end of each lesson, or from the Bonus Ideas (p. 35).

■ Dive into the activities with the kids. Don't be a spectator. The experience will be more successful and rewarding for both you and your students when you play an active role.

■ Have fun with the lessons as you lead your teenagers. Remember, it is Jesus who encourages us to become "like little children." Besides, how often do your kids get *permission* to express their childlike qualities?

■ Be prepared for surprises. In Projects With a Purpose for Youth Ministry lessons, you don't always know which way the lesson will go. Much of your job will be directing kids to stay on task, rather than leading specific activities. As facilitator, you'll be helping kids make their own faith discoveries, rather than directing the results of a specific activity.

■ Encourage new leaders to participate in teaching this course. Projects With a Purpose for Youth Ministry offers an exciting way to give new volunteers a hands-on look at the positive impact youth ministry can have on teenagers.

■ Rely on the Holy Spirit to help you. Remember, only God can give true spiritual insight. Concentrate on your role as the facilitator and trust the Holy Spirit to work in the hearts of your kids.

You Can Do It!

Because Projects With a Purpose for Youth Ministry courses are a different approach to Christian education, leading the lessons might seem a bit scary at first.

That's OK. In fact, it's normal to be a little nervous about a new teaching method. Innovation often requires a risk for the teacher. But hang in there. With the Holy Spirit's guidance and your own desire to make these lessons succeed, great things will happen in your kids' lives.

PUBLICITY PAGE

Grab your teenagers' attention! Photocopy this page, then cut out and paste the clip art of your choice in your church bulletin or newsletter to advertise this course on *Teenagers Teaching Children*. Or photocopy and use the ready-made flier as a bulletin insert. Permission to photocopy this clip art is granted for local church use.

Splash the clip art on posters, fliers, or even postcards! Just add the vital details: the date and time the course begins and where you'll meet.

It's that simple.

A 4-week project where teenagers get to teach the good news to young believers

Come to ....

On ....

At ....

Come discover how you can make a difference in the lives of young believers. We'll plan and teach simple gospel lessons to upper-elementary students.

Planning the Project

Teaching a Bible lesson to upper-elementary students requires careful planning and preparation. This lesson will help teenagers discover effective teaching techniques and formulate plans for teaching the good news.

Students will study Jesus' teaching style and plan upper-elementary lessons using similar methods.

Students will
- explore Jesus' teaching methods,
- refresh themselves on what it was like to be upper-elementary students, and
- plan upper-elementary lessons based on Matthew 5:13-16; Matthew 5:43-47; and Matthew 6:19-24.

Look up the following key Bible passage. Then read the background paragraphs to see how the passage relates to your teenagers. This Scripture will be explored during the Bible study portion of this lesson.

John 16:12 is part of Jesus' "farewell speech" to his disciples.

In this passage, Jesus promises his disciples the Holy Spirit, and advises them of the difficulties they'll face as they spread the good news.

In John 16:12, Jesus says to his disciples, "I have many more things to say to you, but they are too much for you now." Faced with the nearly overwhelming task of getting Jesus' message out to the world, the disciples were no doubt relieved to hear that Jesus would give them only as much information as they could handle.

Today's teenagers live in the information age. Newspapers, television, and other news media constantly bombard them with information. Plus, kids study six or seven different subjects each day at school. Jesus' message in this passage provides a welcome change from the "information overload" they experience each day. Teenagers can also use this passage as a guidepost to how much information to put in their upper-elementary lessons.

LESSON AIM

OBJECTIVES

BIBLE BASIS

JOHN 16:12

Section	Minutes	What Students Will Do	Supplies
Introduction	up to 10	**Good News Teachers**—Get acquainted with one another and with the purpose of this course.	
Bible Study	up to 10	**Jesus, Master Teacher**—Read examples of Jesus' teaching from Luke and John, and identify teaching methods they'll use.	Bibles, paper, pencils
Project Work	up to 10	**Elementary Observations**—Remember what it was like to be upper-elementary students.	
	up to 25	**Action Teams**—Form teams and brainstorm ideas for upper-elementary lessons.	Newsprint, markers, masking tape, "Lesson Structure" handouts (p. 17), "Lesson Plan" handouts (p. 18), Bibles, pencils
Closing	up to 10	**Treasured Teachers**—Share reasons others will be good teachers.	Basket of apples

INTRODUCTION

Note:

During the next four weeks, your students will be teaching upper-elementary children in your church. Plan your class time to coincide with upper-elementary class times, or invite upper-elementary students to join your class during the teaching times indicated in the lessons. If you will be leading this class during the regular church school hour, arrange ahead of time with upper-elementary teachers to allow your students to run a portion of their class time during the coming three weeks.

The Lesson

Good News Teachers
(up to 10 minutes)

Welcome students to the class. Say: **Today we're going to begin a four-week course on Teenagers Teaching Children. But instead of just learning about teaching, we're actually going to practice it ourselves. After we spend some time learning how Jesus taught the gospel, we'll prepare and teach gospel lessons to upper-elementary kids in our church.**

Open with prayer. Then say: **Since we're going to be working closely together on this project, it's important that we all know each other. Let's each introduce ourselves by completing this sentence: "My name is (name). My favorite elementary school teacher was (name of teacher), because..."**

Begin by completing the sentence yourself. After everyone has shared his or her name and favorite teacher, say: **You all liked your teachers for different reasons. Let's keep all those likable qualities in mind as we prepare to try a little teaching ourselves. To help us prepare, let's take a look at a master teacher at work.**

Jesus, Master Teacher

(up to 10 minutes)

Say: Matthew 10:24-25 says, "A student is not better than his teacher, and a servant is not better than his master. A student should be satisfied to become like his teacher; a servant should be satisfied to become like his master."

For the next few weeks, we're going to be serving our master, Jesus, by teaching upper-elementary kids his message. Fortunately, our master is also a master teacher. Jesus is the greatest teacher who ever lived, and we're going to explore some of his teaching methods as we prepare to teach the kids in our church.

Have students look up Mark 4:30-34. When everyone has found the passage, ask a volunteer to read it aloud.

Say: In Jesus' time, many people earned their living by farming, so they would've been familiar with all kinds of seeds. Jesus always told stories and used examples that were relevant to the people he was teaching. Let's practice that technique by creating stories to explain God's kingdom that use relevant examples for people in our time.

Form groups of no more than four. Assign each group one of the following Scripture passages: Matthew 18:21-35; Matthew 20:1-16; Matthew 25:1-13; and Matthew 25:14-30.

Have groups assign the following roles within their foursomes: a reader to read the group's Bible passage; an encourager to encourage everyone to contribute to the group's story; a recorder to write down the story; and a reporter to read the story to the class.

Have the readers read their assigned passages aloud, then have students create their own modern-day versions. After about five minutes, have each group's reporter read his or her group's story to the class.

Ask:

■ **What common objects appeared in your modern-day stories?** (Cars; batteries; flashlights; money.)

■ **How do those objects help people understand the meaning of your stories?** (They know how the objects work; maybe they own some of the objects themselves.)

■ **How are your stories like or unlike the stories you read in the Bible?** (They make the same point, but they use different objects; we changed the situation a little so people could understand better.)

Say: **The teaching stories you created fit into the world of today's listener. Jesus knew the world of his listeners. He also knew their limitations. In John 16:12, Jesus told his disciples, "I have many more things to say to you, but they are too much for you now."** As you're preparing your lessons, you'll need to keep in mind that upper-elementary students don't have the same interests, abilities, or attention spans you do. Let's refresh our memories on what it was like to be upper-elementary students.

Elementary Observations

(up to 10 minutes)

Form trios and have them number off from one to three. Send the ones, twos, and threes to separate areas of the room. Say: **I'm going to read some questions for you to discuss with a partner in your area of the room. If you're a one, answer the questions as if you're a third- or fourth-grader. If you're a two, answer the questions as if you're a fifth-grader. If you're a three, answer the questions as if you're a sixth-grader.**

Ask the following questions one at a time to allow time for like-numbered pairs to discuss them.

■ **What activities are you currently involved in?** (Scouts; music lessons; soccer; T-ball.)

■ **What do you like most about school? What do you like least?** (I like recess the best; I like seeing my friends; I don't like it when my teacher gives us homework; I don't like to take spelling tests.)

■ **How do you feel about the opposite sex?** (I hate boys; girls have cooties; I don't understand why boys don't notice me; I don't understand why girls all go to the restroom together.)

■ **How do you feel about teenagers?** (They're cool because they can drive; I wish they'd pay more attention to me; I can't wait until I turn 13.)

■ **What do you like most about coming to church? What do you like least?** (I like seeing my friends; I like it when our class has a special party; I like playing Tag with the older kids after church; I don't like sitting through the sermon; I don't like memorizing verses.)

After pairs have discussed all the questions, have them return to their original trios and share the responses they discussed with their partners.

Then ask:

■ **Based on what you've heard from others and your own memories of what it was like to be an upper-elementary student, how are these kids different from you?** (They don't like girls; they don't usually have a choice about coming to church; they're interested in playing games; they don't like to sit and listen for very long.)

Say: **As you plan your lessons, keep these characteristics in mind. Consider the world of the kids you'll be teaching, and plan a lesson that will meet kids where they are. You'll have a more enjoyable teaching experience, and you and your students will learn more.**

Now that we've learned a little about our students and about teaching, let's plan some lessons.

Have kids remain in their trios.

Action Teams

(up to 25 minutes)

On a sheet of newsprint, copy the "Teenagers Teaching Children Mission Statement" from page 13. Feel free to adapt this mission statement to fit your group's special characteristics and emphases. Hang the newsprint in the front of the room. Have class members read the mission statement aloud and pledge to uphold its goals. Keep the mission statement posted in your room throughout this course.

Have trios join together to form three groups of six—groups A, B, and C. Assign groups the following Scriptures:

Group A—Matthew 5:13-16 (Be salt and light.)

Group B—Matthew 5:43-47 (Love your enemies.)

Group C—Matthew 6:19-21, 24 (Store up treasure in heaven.)

Say: **For the next three weeks, we'll be teaching upper-elementary classes from the Sermon on the Mount. Jesus covered more territory in that message than most upper-elementary kids can handle, so I've picked out several short, relevant passages for you to teach.**

Read your assigned passage, then brainstorm ideas for teaching that passage to a group of upper-elementary students. Think of common objects you could use to bring your passage to life for kids. Then step back into your third-through sixth-grade mind-sets and think about how your passage could relate to their life experiences.

Give teenagers these examples to jump-start their brainstorming process: For the passage on loving your enemies, teachers could identify possible "enemies" of upper-elementary students. For the passage on storing up treasures, teachers could identify earthly possessions of upper-elementary students. For the passage on salt and light, teachers could identify good things upper-elementary students could do to be lights for other people.

Give groups about seven minutes to brainstorm. As kids are working, travel from group to group to facilitate students' discussions. Then call for their attention and distribute photocopies of the "Lesson Structure" handouts (p. 17) and "Lesson Plan" handouts (p. 18).

Say: **Using the ideas you've discussed, plan a lesson you can teach in about 30 minutes. You'll be teaching your lesson each week for the next three weeks to a different group of upper-elementary students. Next week, group A will teach the third- and fourth-graders; group B will teach the fifth-graders; and group C will teach the sixth-graders. In the weeks that follow, you'll teach the lesson two more times (to the different age groups).**

Your lesson should include a five-minute opening activity, two 10-minute Bible activities, and a five-minute closing activity. The "Lesson Structure" handout lists possible activities for each section.

Within their groups, have students form two teams of three (or fewer if groups are smaller than six). Have each team work on creating one Bible activity and either an opening or a closing activity. Each team will be responsible for teaching the two activities they create. While one team is teaching an activity, the other team will serve as teaching assistants for those activities. Teaching assistants will make sure the teachers

---

Teenagers Teaching Children Mission Statement

We will plan and teach age-appropriate Bible lessons to the upper-elementary students in our church. We will respect the interests, abilities, and limitations of our students. Our lessons will include only material that will encourage our students to know, love, and follow Jesus.

Teacher Tip

If you have more than 18 students in your class, you may want to make arrangements to teach additional upper-elementary classes. Plan on adding one class for each six additional students. Assign additional groups one of the following Scriptures: Matthew 5:21-24; Matthew 6:25-34; Matthew 7:7-11.

If you have fewer than 18 students in your class, form three smaller groups or assign only a couple of the passages and have groups teach combined classes of third- and fourth-graders and fifth- and sixth-graders).

Depending on the class sizes and organization at your church, you may need to choose different age ranges for your students to teach. For example, if you have sixth-graders in your class, you'll need to choose a different age group to teach (such as second-graders).

Or, you could form three student groups from all the upper-elementary kids available for teaching. Then have the three teaching groups (A, B, and C) teach their lessons to a different group each week.

have all the supplies they need and will participate in the activities along with the students to keep things flowing smoothly.

Remind teachers to explain their activities to their teaching assistants before they leave today. Have teenagers record their activities on their "Lesson Plan" handouts.

Assist groups in creating activities as necessary. Some groups may be able to create a complete lesson on their own. Other groups may need substantial help. Encourage kids to come up with their own ideas but be ready to offer the following ideas to help groups complete their lessons:

Ideas for group A: Matthew 5:13-16 (Be salt and light.)

■ Form two groups. Serve one group of kids unsalted food such as french fries or popcorn. Serve the other group the same foods, only with salt. Talk about the difference.

■ Hide a snack and have kids try to find it in the dark. The snack is like God's reward for those who follow him. People won't be able to find God's good reward without the light of our good actions.

■ Turn off the lights in the room and have kids take turns picking an object to look at. Have the rest of the kids try to guess the object. Then play again, only this time have the student shine a flashlight at the object he or she is looking at. Talk about how the light of our good actions can lead people straight to God.

■ Give kids each a candle. Light your candle, then say one good deed you'll do this week. Have kids light each other's candles as they share good deeds they'll do. Close in prayer.

Ideas for group B: Matthew 5:43-47 (Love your enemies.)

■ Create two or three situations where kids might have a hard time loving someone. Have kids work in groups to read the situations and decide what they'd do. Have them act out their responses for the rest of the class.

■ Play Hug Tag. Form two teams and call one team the neighbors and the other team the enemies. Give the enemies sheets of red adhesive dots and tell them to make enemies out of the neighbors by inflicting "wounds" on them with the red adhesive dots. If a neighbor hugs an enemy before the enemy wounds him or her, that enemy becomes a neighbor. Play until everyone becomes enemies or everyone becomes neighbors. Talk about how love can spread from person to person.

■ Divide the passage into one- or two-sentence sections. Assign each section of the passage to a group of two to four students, and have them come up with a way to act it out. "Love your enemies" could be acted out by one student hugging another student with clinched fists and a snarling face, for example. Teachers and teaching assistants may need to help kids think of ideas. Have kids perform their Scripture drama for an adult class.

■ Have kids each think of someone who's hurt them or been mean to them in the past week. Distribute adhesive bandages and have kids each write the name of that person on the inside of the bandage. Close in prayer, then have kids wear the bandages on their arms to remind them to pray for those who hurt them.

Ideas for group C: Matthew 6:19-21, 24 (Store up treasure in heaven.)

■ Play a game like Capture the Flag or Steal the Bacon, then talk about what it would be like if their possessions were stolen.

■ Have a treasure hunt. Open a roll of quarters and hide them all around the room. Also hide a small Bible. Have kids look for the treasure, but don't say what the treasure is. See if kids find the Bible.

■ Have kids each draw a picture of their favorite possession. Then have the teaching assistants come in dressed like robbers and steal all the pictures. Talk about how temporary our worldly possessions are.

■ Make sure each student has a Bible. You may need to borrow some from the church. Have kids create book covers for their Bibles to remind them that the Bible is God's treasure. Suggest images such as Bibles in treasure chests or a moth inside a red circle with a slash through it. Provide a small heart pattern and have kids include a heart somewhere in their designs. Have kids put the covers on their Bibles, then form a circle.

Give each student a red construction paper heart cut from the heart pattern. Have them each find the heart on the book cover of the person next to them, then say, "(Name of person), your heart will be where your treasure is." Provide an extra supply of red hearts for kids to stick on their possessions at home to remind them of this lesson.

Allow as much time as possible for kids to plan their lessons. About 10 minutes before your class ends, have kids stop their work and join you for the closing activity.

Table Talk

The "Table Talk" activity in this course helps teenagers explore the impact that caring teachers have had on their Christian development. If you choose to use the "Table Talk" activity, this is a good time to show students the "Table Talk" handout (p. 19). Ask them to spend time with their parents completing it.

Before kids leave, give them each the "Table Talk" handout to take home or tell them you'll be sending it to their parents. Tell kids to be prepared to report next week on their experiences with the handout.

Treasured Teachers

(up to 10 minutes)

Form a circle and place a basket of apples in the center. Make sure you have enough apples for each student to have one. Say: **We're about to embark on a great adventure as we teach the good news** to upper-elementary kids. Take a few moments to reflect on the things you've learned and the work your team has done to prepare your lesson. Think about the people on your team and what each of you will contribute to your teaching experience.

Allow kids a few moments to think, then continue: **Take an apple from the basket in the center and present it to one of your team members and tell why you think that person will be a treasured teacher. For example, you might say, "Pete, you'll be a treasured teacher because of your enthusiasm" or "Sue, you'll be a treasured teacher because of your sense of humor." If the person you're thinking of has already been given an apple, give one to someone else on your team.**

When all the apples have been distributed, have kids say, "Go, team!" together, then bite into their apples. Close in prayer by asking God to guide kids as they teach.

Save the lesson plans for use in the coming weeks. If kids want to do additional work on their lessons or study them outside of class, make photocopies of the lesson plans for their use. Keep the originals.

Allow a few minutes at the end of class to discuss their plans for next week. Determine what needs to be done before next week's class, and assign responsibilities as needed to assure the necessary work is completed. Responsibilities might include setting up classrooms, making name tags, gathering supplies, and so on. Assign as many of the responsibilities as possible to the kids, but help out as appropriate.

If You Still Have Time...

Who Are You?—Have teenagers interview upper-elementary kids and teachers after church to help them know what to expect next week.

Any Questions?—Jesus was an asker, not a teller. Have kids study Jesus' questions by picking one of the gospels and highlighting all the questions Jesus asked. Encourage kids to ask questions when they teach, using questions similar to the ones Jesus asked.

LESSON STRUCTURE

Your upper-elementary lesson should include an opening activity, two Bible activities, and a closing activity. Each activity should focus on the point of your lesson. Refer to the descriptions below for possible activities to include in each section of the lesson. Ask your leader if you have questions about any of the activities described on this handout.

Opening

This activity should quickly introduce kids to the topic you'll be teaching. Possible opening activities include
- games,
- large group activities, and
- learning stations.

Bible Activities

In these activities, kids should experience something, talk about the experience, then connect the experience to their lives. In at least one activity, have children read or listen to your lesson's Bible passage. Possible Bible activities include
- games,
- discussing or acting out responses to situations,
- craft activities,
- acting out Bible passages,
- mock game shows,
- creative prayers, and
- affirmation activities.

Closing

Closing activities should wrap up the lesson and remind kids about what they've learned. The closing activity is also a good time to have kids commit to putting the lesson into practice this week. Possible closing activities include
- creative prayers,
- affirmation activities,
- songs, and
- reminder crafts.

LESSON PLAN

Lesson Title
_____

Lesson Scripture
_____

Main Point Kids Should Learn
_____

Opening Activity
Time required:
Description of activity:

Supplies needed:

Teachers:
Teaching assistants:

Bible Activity 1
Time required:
Description of activity:

Supplies needed:

Teachers:
Teaching assistants:

Bible Activity 2
Time required:
Description of activity:

Supplies needed:

Teachers:
Teaching assistants:

Closing Activity
Time required:
Description of activity:

Supplies needed:

Teachers:
Teaching assistants:

Table Talk

To the Parent: We're involved in a senior high project at church called *Teenagers Teaching Children.* Students are creating 30-minute Bible lessons based on the Sermon on the Mount to teach to upper-elementary students in the church. We'd like you and your teenager to talk about your experiences with teaching and learning the gospel message. Use this "Table Talk" page to help you do that.

Parent

- Describe your favorite childhood Sunday school teacher.
- What are the most memorable Bible lessons you were taught in your youth?
- What do you think is the most important message kids should learn about Jesus?

Teenager

- What are you most looking forward to about teaching the good news to upper elementary kids?
- What aspects of the gospel are most relevant to your generation?
- What qualities make a person a good teacher?

Parent and teenager

- How do you learn best?
- What is the gospel, the good news, that Jesus wants us to share?
- How has your understanding of the gospel changed over the years?
- What could others learn about the gospel by observing your life?

Read Psalm 119:1-16 together. How can studying God's Word make you a good teacher? Why is it important to pass Jesus' teachings on to the next generation? How can you be more loyal in following God's teaching?

If you haven't already done so, tell each other how you'll teach by example this week. Pray that God will help you live by his teachings and pass those teachings along to others.

LESSON 2

What Can Kids Learn?

As your students approach teaching their first lesson, they may be nervous or unsure about how well their students will grasp the messages they'll be teaching. But as they present their lessons, your teenagers will discover that upper-elementary children are often eager to explore their faith.

LESSON AIM

Students will discover the importance of teaching kids the good news.

OBJECTIVES

Students will
■ remember things about the gospel they learned as children,
■ discuss the importance of teaching the gospel to younger Christians, and
■ teach the good news to upper-elementary students.

BIBLE BASIS

PSALM 78:1-7

Look up the following key Bible passage. Then read the background paragraphs to see how the passage relates to your teenagers. This Scripture will be explored during the Bible study portion of this lesson.

Psalm 78:1-7 urges the Israelite people to tell their children about the great things God has done.

The author of this psalm knew all too well the unfortunate results of neglecting to pass on God's message. Israel's history reads like a broken record, as time after time the people forgot what God had done, then turned away from him. Verses 3 and 4 affirm that the current generation was determined not to repeat the mistakes of the past. They would pass God's message on to their children—even to the children not yet born.

The psalmist's message has passed from generation to generation, and today it falls on your teenagers' ears. As they prepare to teach their lessons, use this passage to remind teenagers that they're part of God's plan for keeping the message alive. Not only will their teaching instruct a new generation in God's ways, but it will also bear fruit in their own lives as they learn old lessons through new eyes.

Section	Minutes	What Students Will Do	Supplies
Introduction	up to 10	**Promotion Day**—Remember things they learned at church.	Newsprint, markers
Project Work	up to 30	**Teaching Teams**—Teach prepared lessons to an upper-elementary class.	Completed "Lesson Plan" handouts (p.18) from lesson 1, lesson supplies, Bibles
	up to 10	**The Next Step**—Adjust their lessons as necessary and gather supplies for next week.	"Lesson Plan" handouts (p.18), pencils
Bible Study	up to 10	**Teach the Children**—Discuss the importance of passing God's message to a new generation.	Bibles
Closing	up to 5	**The Praises of the Lord**—Recount the group's history with God.	Bible

The Lesson

Before the lesson: Your students will be meeting together before and after their teaching times to participate in the rest of the lesson's activities. Each teaching team will be teaching a separate group of children, but at the same time as the other teams. Teams will rotate weekly, teaching their message to a different group each week.

Promotion Day
(up to 10 minutes)

Welcome students to the class. Say: **Today, in our second week of this course on** *Teenagers Teaching Children,* **we're going to teach our first lesson to upper-elementary kids.**

Welcome visitors and class members who weren't here last week. Have a volunteer explain what the class is working on. Invite guests to join the teaching teams as teaching assistants.

Post six sheets of newsprint around the room. On the top of each sheet, write one of the following words or phrases: "preschool," "1st–2nd grade," "3rd–4th grade," "5th–6th grade," "junior high," and "high school."

Have students write on each sheet of newsprint things they learned about God, Jesus, or the Bible when they were that age. After about five minutes, call kids together.

Have volunteers read each of the lists. Then say: **Look at the third- through sixth-grade lists. The children you'll be**

INTRODUCTION

teaching will know many of these things. Now look at the high school list. What's the most important thing you've learned in class this year? Pick something from the list or tell about something else that stands out in your mind.

Go around the room and have kids share the most important things they've learned in class this year. Then say: **With the Holy Spirit's help, the lessons you're about to teach could be the most important things these kids learn this year. For some who don't come to church regularly, your lesson may be the first time they've heard the gospel. Let's pray and ask God to go with us as we teach.**

Have a volunteer pray.

Table Talk Follow-Up

If you sent the "Table Talk" handout (p. 19) to parents last week, discuss students' reactions to the activity. Ask volunteers to share what they learned from the discussion with their parents.

Teaching Teams

(up to 30 minutes)

Have teenagers go to their assigned classrooms to teach the lessons they planned last week using their "Lesson Plan" handouts (p. 18). Assist as necessary to make sure kids have the supplies and any help they need. Circulate between the rooms to observe part of each of the three lessons.

When groups have completed teaching their lessons, call them together and review their lesson plans for next week's class. Have groups each give a brief report of their experiences by having volunteers complete the following sentences for the whole class:

■ **The thing that surprised me most about today's teaching experience was...**

■ **I was most impressed when...**

Thank your students for their willingness to reach out to younger children with the gospel message. Then say: **Before we dive into our brief Bible study, let's take a few moments to explore ways we can improve our lessons for next week.**

The Next Step

(up to 10 minutes)

Have volunteers tell what worked and what didn't work in their lessons. Then have teaching teams meet together and spend up to 10 minutes discussing how they'll adjust their lessons for the coming week.

PROJECT WORK

Teacher Tip

If possible, have the regular upper-elementary teacher observe the lessons, as kids in the class will be less likely to misbehave if the regular teacher is present.

As you observe your students teaching, watch for any discipline problems in the class. Upper-elementary kids will likely be excited by your teenagers' presence and may act inappropriately. If teenagers seem to be having trouble getting or keeping kids' attention, suggest they use an attention-getting signal such as flashing the lights to signal it's time to be quiet and listen. If the problem seems to be one or two rowdy kids, encourage teenagers to seek the help of the regular teacher to control the rambunctious students.

Ask kids to dump ideas that didn't work, in favor of new ones. Have them write their new ideas on their "Lesson Plan" handouts (p. 18), then plan appropriately for next week. Remind students that sometimes it's difficult to tell how God will use their efforts.

Help kids assign responsibilities as needed to assure they complete the necessary work before next week's lesson.

Be prepared to spend time with kids after class or during the week to help them modify their lessons based on today's teaching experience.

Teach the Children

(up to 10 minutes)

Form groups of no more than four. Have group members take turns completing the following sentence: "Something I learned today about teaching children is . . ."

Students might say things such as, "Third-grade boys don't like to sit next to third-grade girls" or "Fourth- and fifth-graders seem to enjoy active activities most."

Have volunteers tell the class their group's responses. Then have the person wearing the most green in each group read aloud Psalm 78:1-7. Ask the following questions, allowing time for discussion after each one. Have the person in each group who taught the oldest children report the group's answers to the first question, the next oldest report answers to the second question, and so on.

Ask:

■ **What would our world be like if no one passed on the things they knew about God to the next generation?** (Violent; crazy; someone would have figured out that there was a God because of all the perfect things he's created.)

■ **This passage doesn't specify any qualifications required for teaching children about God. What do you think would make the author of this passage a good teacher of children?** (He seems enthusiastic; he was inspired; he must be really dedicated if he even wants to tell unborn children about God.)

■ **Why should we teach the gospel message to the next generation while they're young instead of waiting until they grow up?** (So they can get excited about God early; kids are willing to listen and sometimes adults aren't; Jesus didn't turn children away, so we shouldn't either.)

Say: When we teach the gospel to the next generation, we also reinforce it in our own lives. As you prepare for your lessons next week, read over your Scripture passage each day and look for ways to apply it to your life. Ask God to give you the psalmist's enthusiasm for sharing the good news with children.

BIBLE STUDY

Teacher Tip

Teenagers will get more out of this activity if groups include no more than two members of the same teaching team.

The Praises of the Lord

(up to 5 minutes)

Say: **Psalm 78 records all the good things God did for Israel. Let's create our own psalm of praise for all the good things God has done for our group.**

Begin with the youngest students in your class, then invite older students to contribute as you trace the history of God's involvement with your group. If kids have trouble getting started, read them one or two specific examples from Psalm 78. Kids might say things like, "God brought more people to our group" or "God taught us to love each other."

Close in prayer, asking God to help you remember all the great things he's done.

Allow a few minutes at the end of class to discuss kids' teaching plans for next week. Determine what needs to be done before next week's class and make assignments accordingly.

If You Still Have Time . . .

Try This One—Have one or more of the teaching teams lead the class through an activity from their upper-elementary lessons. Then form new groups and have kids discuss what worked well and how the activity could be improved.

What Would You Do?—Invite one of the upper-elementary teachers to a question-and-answer time. Have the teacher describe how he or she got involved in teaching, then offer tips to help kids succeed in their upper-elementary lessons. Allow time for kids to ask questions.

What Can Kids Teach Us?

As your students enter their second week of teaching the good news, they're probably focused on the material they've prepared to teach their upper-elementary students. But teaching is not a one-way street. Any good teacher knows that he or she is a learner as well as a teacher.

This lesson will help teenagers discover that they can learn from, as well as teach, the upper-elementary children in your church.

LESSON AIM

Students will explore Jesus' teachings about becoming like children.

OBJECTIVES

Students will
- use children's toys to describe their relationships with God,
- explore ways Jesus taught and interacted with children,
- identify childlike characteristics required for following God, and
- teach the good news to upper-elementary students.

BIBLE BASIS

MATTHEW 18:1-5
1 JOHN 5:1-5

Look up the following key Bible passages. Then read the background paragraphs to see how the passages relate to your teenagers. These Scriptures will be explored during the Bible study portion of this lesson.

Matthew 18:1-5 shows us Jesus' love for children.

In this passage, Jesus tells his followers that they must humble themselves and become like little children in order to enter the kingdom of heaven. But what does it mean to become like children? Children make new discoveries each day. And although they may fall, they're always willing to pick themselves up and keep going. Above all, children are willing to trust.

Your students have only recently left childhood. They're nearly adults now, and most would prefer not to be reminded of the childish or immature things they did when they were children. This passage can remind teenagers of the important difference between being *childish* and becoming *childlike*.

1 John 5:1-5 talks about the privileges of being a child of God.

This passage reminds us that, in God's eyes, we're all still children. We don't have to know or understand sophisticated theological principles to be in God's family. Rather, this passage points out that "everyone who believes that Jesus is the Christ" is God's child.

The teenagers in your church may think they're light-years ahead of their upper-elementary students in their faith development. Yet even the youngest children can relate to the basics of faith. Use this passage to encourage teenagers to focus on the essentials of their faith—believing in Jesus and obeying God's commands.

THIS LESSON AT A GLANCE

Section	Minutes	What Students Will Do	Supplies
Introduction	up to 10	**Building Blocks**—Compare blocks and other children's toys to their relationship with God.	Bag of children's toys, including blocks, cars, and dolls
Bible Study	up to 10	**Let the Children Come**—Discover the importance of childlike faith.	Bibles
Project Work	up to 30	**Teaching Teams**—Teach prepared lessons to an upper-elementary class.	Completed "Lesson Plan" handouts (p. 18) from lesson 1, lesson supplies, Bibles
	up to 10	**The Next Step**—Adjust their lessons as necessary and gather supplies for next week.	"Lesson Plan" handouts (p. 18), pencils
Closing	up to 5	**Faith of a Child**—Pray as they share observations about childlike faith.	

The Lesson

INTRODUCTION

Building Blocks

(up to 10 minutes)

Before class, borrow some toys from the preschool or nursery departments in your church. Put the toys in a large paper sack.

Open with prayer. Welcome guests and visitors and have a class member explain to them what the class is working on. Invite guests to join the teaching teams as teaching assistants.

Form a circle. Pass around the sack of toys and invite each student to take one. When the sack comes back to you, say: **Think of one way your relationship with God is like the toy you're holding in your hand. For example, if you're holding a** toy car, you might say, "God is in the driver's seat in my life" or if you're holding a block, you might say, "I try to build my life on God." Take a moment to think, then share your thoughts with someone next to you.

Allow time for partners to share their thoughts about the toys. Then have them discuss the following questions:

■ **How easy or hard was it to compare the toy to your relationship with God? Explain.** (Hard because God is so awesome and my toy was silly; easy because it reminded me of things I need to work on in my relationship with God.)

■ **How has your relationship with God changed since the time you were young enough to play with these toys?** (I know a lot more about God now; I trust God more; I put more work into the relationship now.)

Say: **Most of us know more about God now than we did when we were young children. However, there are some things about God that children seem to understand best of all. Before we teach our upper-elementary lessons today, let's take a look at Scriptures about childlike faith.**

Let the Children Come

(up to 10 minutes)

Form two groups by having the kids with birthdays in January through June stand on the right side of the room and kids with birthdays in July through December stand on the left side (even out the groups if necessary). Call the group on the right side "disciples" and the group on the left side "Pharisees."

Say: **The Pharisees and disciples have been talking about the kingdom of heaven. Both groups feel pretty good about themselves and think they'll rank pretty high in the pecking order.**

Pharisees, you know you've got a sure thing because you've obeyed every law on the books for all your lives. Disciples, you're pretty sure you'll ace out the Pharisees since you've left jobs and families to serve in Jesus' ministry.

You have one minute to convince each other why you'll be the greatest in the kingdom of heaven. Go!

After one minute, have kids stop their discussions or arguments and find a partner from the other side of the room. Have pairs look up Matthew 18:1-5 and discuss the following questions:

■ **How is Jesus' point of view different than the arguments you just heard?** (He doesn't count all the things people have done; great doesn't mean the same thing to him as it did to the disciples.)

■ **What do you think Jesus meant when he said we must become like little children?** (That we should trust him more; we shouldn't be so concerned with status and power.)

■ **What's the difference between childlike qualities and childish qualities?** (Childlike qualities are positive; childish qualities are the negative traits of children.)

After kids have discussed the questions, ask volunteers to share the responses they discussed with their partners. Then have someone read 1 John 5:1-5 aloud.

Say: **We can learn a lot about faith from the children in our church. Although it's important to keep maturing in our spiritual lives, our experiences with teaching children will remind us not to neglect the essentials of our faith. The love for God and belief in his son, Jesus, that we learned as children will remain with us our whole lives.**

As you interact with your upper-elementary students today, listen closely to their responses. You'll probably learn a lot about childlike faith.

PROJECT WORK

Teacher Tip

If any of the upper-elementary classes your kids are teaching have fewer than six students, consider combining classes and having each teaching group present one Bible activity.

Teacher Tip

Once again, if possible, have the regular upper-elementary teacher observe the lessons, as kids will be less likely to misbehave if the regular teacher is present. See the "Teacher Tip" on page 22 for ideas on solving discipline problems.

Teaching Teams
(up to 30 minutes)

Have teenagers go to their assigned classrooms to teach the lessons they planned last week using their "Lesson Plan" handouts (p. 18). Assist your student teachers as necessary to make sure they have the supplies and any help they need. Encourage teaching assistants to pay special attention to kids' responses and make a mental note of childlike faith characteristics they observe. Circulate between the rooms to observe part of each of the three lessons.

When teams have completed teaching their lessons, call them together and review the lesson plans for next week's class. Have each group give a brief report of their experiences by having volunteers complete the following sentences for the whole class:
■ **The thing that surprised me most about today's teaching experience was...**
■ **I was most impressed when...**
■ **Some childlike qualities I observed were...**
■ **Some childish qualities I observed were...**
Thank your students for their willingness to reach out to younger children with the gospel message.

The Next Step
(up to 10 minutes)

Have volunteers tell what worked and what didn't work in their lessons. Then have teaching teams meet together and spend up to 10 minutes discussing how they'll adjust their lessons for the coming week.

Have kids dump ideas that didn't work, in favor of new ones. Have them write their new ideas on their "Lesson Plan" handouts (p.18) and plan appropriately for next week. Remind students that sometimes it's difficult to tell how much kids really get out of a class and that it's OK if things didn't go perfectly.

Help kids assign responsibilities as needed to assure they complete the necessary work before next week's lesson.

Be prepared to spend time with kids after class or during the week to help them modify their lessons based on today's teaching experiences.

Faith of a Child

(up to 5 minutes)

Form a circle. Say: **Let's close with a prayer that expresses our thanks to God for renewing our childlike faith. I'll open, and when I say "Help our faith to be..." we'll go around the circle and each contribute one word that describes the childlike qualities you'd like to develop in your faith life. If someone says the quality you were thinking of, it's OK to repeat it.**

Give kids a moment to think, then begin the prayer. Pray: **Dear God, thank you for embracing us all as your children. We thank you for the lessons we've learned from the faith of our upper-elementary students. Help our faith to be..."**

Kids might suggest qualities such as enthusiastic, adventuresome, sincere, innocent, trusting, and so on. After each person in the circle has suggested a childlike quality, close by saying "amen" together. Then sing "Jesus Loves Me."

If You Still Have Time...

Hey, God?—Have kids list questions they had about God when they were young children, then write down the answers they've discovered as they've grown older. Then have them write letters to God that ask the questions they're struggling with today.

Faith Tunes—Play songs about children or childlike faith by contemporary Christian artists such as "The Warrior Is a Child" by Twila Paris. Form pairs and have kids discuss the childlike qualities mentioned in each song.

4

Harvesting the Seeds

OK. During the first week, Jesse put a worm in Jonathan's pocket. And in the second week, Sally tried to escape by climbing out of the window. By now, your teenagers may be wondering whether their teaching efforts are worth the pain and frustration. This lesson will help kids focus on the potential positive results of their teaching.

LESSON AIM

Students will reflect on their teaching experiences and discover ways to encourage kids to grow in their faith.

OBJECTIVES

Students will
- compare their teaching experience to sowing and harvesting,
- teach the good news to upper-elementary students,
- reflect on their teaching experiences, and
- plant seeds to remind them to maintain the relationships they've developed with their upper-elementary students.

BIBLE BASIS

LUKE 8:4-15

Look up the following key Bible passage. Then read the background paragraphs to see how the passage relates to your teenagers. This Scripture will be explored during the Bible study portion of this lesson.

In **Luke 8:4-15**, Jesus tells a parable about planting seed.

In this familiar parable, Jesus compares spreading the good news to a farmer planting seed. Depending on where the seed falls, the message of God may thrive and grow or remain dormant. If only the farmer knew the nature of the soil, he could plant all the seed in good soil where it would thrive and grow. But the farmer is a farmer, not a soil scientist. Studying the soil is not his responsibility—planting seeds is.

Rather than hoarding the seed for fear that it might fall in bad soil, the farmer scatters it far and wide in the hope that some of it will reach the good soil and survive, and perhaps even thrive.

By the end of this lesson, your teenagers will have completed potentially trying, but rewarding, teaching experiences. They may wonder if any of their gospel seeds have landed in good soil. Use this passage to help them realize that God can use the seeds they've planted in mighty ways.

Section	Minutes	What Students Will Do	Supplies
Introduction	up to 10	**Sow It, Grow It!**—Imagine what kind of plants would grow from kitchen utensil seeds.	Kitchen utensils and dishes, newsprint, tape, markers
Project Work	up to 30	**Teaching Teams**—Teach prepared lessons to an upper-elementary class.	Completed "Lesson Plan" handouts (p.18) from lesson 1, lesson supplies, Bibles
Bible Study	up to 15	**Soil Samples**—Read the parable of the sower and identify potential thorns and rocks in their students' lives.	Bibles, paper, pencils
Closing	up to 10	**One Hundred Fold**—Plant "gospel seeds" for upper-elementary students.	Seeds, soil, plastic cups, permanent-ink markers, thank-you notes, pencils

The Lesson

Sow It, Grow It!
(up to 10 minutes)

Before class, gather kitchen utensils and dishes from the church kitchen. Place the utensils on the floor around the edge of the room. Tape a sheet of newsprint to the wall above each utensil.

Open with prayer. Welcome guests and visitors and have a class member explain to them what the class is working on. Invite guests to join the teaching teams as teaching assistants.

Form trios and have each group choose a kitchen utensil. Say: **When you were younger, did anyone ever tell you that if you swallowed a watermelon seed, a watermelon plant would grow in your stomach? Well, we're going to go back to those younger days for this next activity.**

Imagine what would happen if we planted these utensils, instead. What kind of plant would grow from a spatula, a measuring cup, or a wooden spoon? Would it be a bush, a flower, a tree, or some combination? Work with the others in your trio to design a plant for your utensil. Draw your design on the newsprint near your utensil.

Encourage kids to have fun and be creative as they design their utensil plants. After a couple of minutes, call time and have groups present their plant drawings to the class. After groups briefly discuss the following questions, have volunteers from each group share their group's insights with the whole class.

Ask:

■ **How did you determine what kind of plant would grow from these utensil seeds?** (We used a similar design; we figured a spoon would grow into a huge tree.)

■ **Think about your current habits and priorities. What kind of seeds are growing in your life?** (Seeds of friendship; power flowers; my seeds are being invaded by bookworms.)

■ **How long have those seeds been growing? When were they planted?** (My sports seeds have been growing since I made the winning touchdown on my fifth-grade football team; my mom planted my study seeds when she realized my grades might not be good enough to get into college.)

Say: **Today we come to the end of our project and our exploration of teaching and learning. Let's make our last lessons the best yet as we sow the last round of seeds in these upper-elementary children.**

Teaching Teams

(up to 30 minutes)

Have teenagers go to their assigned classrooms to teach their final lessons using their "Lesson Plan" handouts (p. 18). Assist as necessary to make sure they have the supplies and any help they need. Circulate between the rooms to observe part of each of the three lessons.

When groups have completed teaching their lessons, call them together for the Bible study and closing activities. Let kids keep their "Lesson Plan" sheets as momentos of their teaching experiences, or collect them and keep them in a scrapbook in your room.

Have groups each give a brief report of their experiences by having volunteers complete the following sentences for the whole class:

■ **The thing that surprised me most about today's teaching experience was** . . .

■ **I was most impressed when** . . .

■ **Through this lesson, I believe we've planted the seeds of** . . .

Thank your students again for their willingness to explore the world of teaching through this project.

Soil Samples

(up to 15 minutes)

Have kids stay with their teaching teams and read the parable of the sower from Luke 8:4-15.

After groups discuss the following questions, have volunteers share their group's answers with the whole class.

Ask:

■ **What thorns and rocks keep God's Word from taking root in your lives?** (Peer pressure; worries about college; wanting to sleep in on Sunday mornings.)

■ **What thorns and rocks do you think keep God's Word**

Teacher Tip

Encourage teenagers to ask their students what they remember from the previous weeks' lessons. Remind kids to thank the upper-elementary kids and their teachers for letting them take over their classes for a few weeks.

Teacher Tip

If any of the upper-elementary classes your kids are teaching have fewer than six students, consider combining classes and having each teaching group present one Bible activity.

from taking root in your upper-elementary students' lives? (Too much Nintendo; parents divorcing; moving to a new school.)

Then have kids record on a slip of paper whether the class they taught today seemed like roadside, rocky, thorny, or good soil.

After everyone has written down a soil type, have kids reveal their choices. Have kids form new groups according to their soil types. You may need to even out the groups if most kids choose the same soil type.

Say: **Without mentioning names of specific students, talk with others in your group about why you chose that particular type of soil to represent your teaching experience. Then talk about ways you can help "fertilize" that soil so the gospel seeds can grow.**

Allow about five minutes for soil groups to discuss their experiences. Afterward, have volunteers share their group's suggestions for helping the seeds grow.

Wrap up the Bible study by reading 1 Corinthians 3:6-9. Say: **We can water and fertilize all we want, but only God can make our seeds grow. As we close our teaching experience, let's pray that God will grow good fruit out of the seeds we've planted these past few weeks.**

One Hundred Fold

(up to 10 minutes)

CLOSING

Give each student several seeds and some soil in a plastic cup. Have kids plant their seeds, then form pairs with someone not from their teaching team. Provide permanent-ink markers as needed.

Say: **Think about all the upper-elementary kids you met during this course. Pick one student who really made an impact on your life. Maybe it was a student who was a natural leader, a boy who couldn't sit still, or a girl who seemed painfully shy.**

Tell your partner what it was you noticed about that student, then write the student's first name on the outside of your seed cup.

After partners have written the names on their seed cups, place the cups in a window or other sunny location in your room to remind you of your teaching experiences. Don't forget to water them!

Gather in a circle. Say: **1 Corinthians 3:9 says that we are all God's workers, working together. Because of the work you've done these past few weeks, the upper-elementary students in our church have grown closer to God. Let's take a few moments to celebrate the work we've done.**

Have teenagers complete the following sentence about the person on their right: "I appreciated the work you did..." Kids might say things like, "I appreciated the work you did to bring our first class under control" or "I appreciated the work you did at home to make our lessons a success."

After everyone has been affirmed, add your own affirmations about the group's willingness to work together on a unique and challenging project.

Have students write thank-you notes to the upper-elementary kids and teachers. Deliver them after class.

If You Still Have Time ...

Faith Planter—Have kids plant all their seeds in a planter box or, if you live in a mild climate, outdoors on the church grounds. Have someone make a "Faith Patch" sign to let people know what's growing. Encourage kids to care for the plants as a reminder that God calls us to care for the faith-growth of children.

Planted Thanks—Have kids each write a thank-you note to the upper-elementary teachers who shared their classes. Put all the notes in a pitcher or watering pot and deliver them to the teachers with the label: "Thank you for sharing your 'seeds.' Please keep watering them."

Bonus Ideas

Bonus Scriptures—The lessons focus on a select few Scripture passages, but if you'd like to incorporate more Bible readings into a lesson, here are some suggestions:

■ Matthew 21:14-16 (You have taught children and babies to sing praises.)

■ 1 John 3:1-3 (We're children of God.)

■ 2 Timothy 3:16 (All Scripture is useful for teaching.)

■ Deuteronomy 6:1-9 (Teach children to love God.)

Taping the Good News—If you or someone in your church has a video camera, videotape your students in action. Tape each teaching team for about 10 minutes during the first week's lesson. Then watch the video after class to get helpful tips for the next week. Or tape each teaching team for an entire lesson. Then after the last lesson, let kids see each other in action. They'll enjoy seeing other teams' teaching ideas.

What Have You Learned?—Have kids invite teachers from your church to participate in a panel discussion about the teaching experience. Have teenagers ask questions such as:

■ What's the most difficult thing about teaching?

■ What's the most rewarding thing about teaching?

■ What have you learned most from your teaching experience?

■ What advice would you give someone who is considering teaching in the church?

Teenagers Teaching Children 2—If your teenagers enjoyed this project, try another round of teaching. If you have a small group, use the additional passages from the Sermon on the Mount listed in the first lesson. Other fun-to-teach topics could include the Ten Commandments or the fruit of the Spirit. Or let teenagers pick their own topics this time, but make sure they choose something simple enough for upper-elementary kids to understand.

Superstar Teachers—During each of the three teaching weeks of this project, highlight one teaching team as "Teachers of the Week." During the first lesson, take photos of all three teams preparing for their lessons. Then, for each of the following weeks, create and display a "Superstar Teachers" poster highlighting one of the teams.

MEETINGS AND MORE

Choose materials for your posters that will make people stop and take notice, such as neon poster board, sequins, or glitter. List team members' names on the poster, and glue on two or three snapshots of the team. Put the poster in a stairwell, fellowship hall, or other prominent place where church members can see the good work your students are doing.

Teacher Follow-Up—If you have students who really enjoyed their teaching experiences, encourage them to find out more about teaching in the church by checking out one of the following resources:
- *Becoming a Treasured Teacher* (Jody Capehart, Scripture Press)
- *Why Nobody Learns Much of Anything at Church: And How to Fix It* (Thom and Joani Schultz, Group Publishing)

Big Brothers and Sisters—Encourage kids to help their upper-elementary students grow by "adopting" them. Help teenagers plan regular times to spend with their new younger siblings. Include plenty of fun times—your teenagers' actions and attitudes during casual interactions may teach kids the gospel even better than their classroom lessons.

Teacher Tryouts—Use this course for other adults in your church who might be interested in teaching children. Allow them the opportunity to try it out for a few weeks.

PARTY PLEASER

Next Generation Party—Have a costume party where kids come dressed as people from past or future generations. Play games from the past and games you think might be played in the future.

Choose a location where you can decorate several rooms in past and future styles and have kids create posters of Deuteronomy 6:4-5 to match the style of each room. During the party, spend time in prayer asking God to bless your efforts to teach the good news to the next generation.

RETREAT IDEAS

Teaching Mini-Retreat—Instead of teaching your lessons during class, plan a daylong mini-retreat for the upper-elementary kids you'll be teaching. Have your teaching groups rotate, teaching their messages to the children throughout the mini-retreat.

Provide snacks and lunch for teenagers and their students. Include planned recreation and free time along with the lessons you'll be teaching.

Return-to-Childhood Retreat—Turn teenagers' attention to their childlike faith by calling them back to childhood for a one- or two-day retreat. Invite kids to bring their favorite toys or stuffed animals along, and play favorite childhood games. If your retreat site has a TV and VCR, you might even watch cartoons or Disney movies.

Have kids discuss the childlike qualities they have and explore which qualities they want to improve.

Close the retreat by reading and discussing Jesus' attitude toward the children in Mark 10:13-16. This retreat provides a fun way for teenagers to re-enter the world of the upper-elementary students they'll be teaching in this course.

CURRICULUM REORDER—TOP PRIORITY

Order now to prepare for your upcoming Sunday school classes, youth ministry meetings, and weekend retreats! Each book includes all teacher and student materials—plus photocopiable handouts—for any size class . . . for just $8.99 each!

FOR SENIOR HIGH:

1 & 2 Corinthians: Christian Discipleship, ISBN 1-55945-230-7

Angels, Demons, Miracles & Prayer, ISBN 1-55945-235-8

Changing the World, ISBN 1-55945-236-6

Christians in a Non-Christian World, ISBN 1-55945-224-2

Christlike Leadership, ISBN 1-55945-231-5

Communicating With Friends, ISBN 1-55945-228-5

Counterfeit Religions, ISBN 1-55945-207-2

Dating Decisions, ISBN 1-55945-215-3

Dealing With Life's Pressures, ISBN 1-55945-232-3

Deciphering Jesus' Parables, ISBN 1-55945-237-4

Exodus: Following God, ISBN 1-55945-226-9

Exploring Ethical Issues, ISBN 1-55945-225-0

Faith for Tough Times, ISBN 1-55945-216-1

Forgiveness, ISBN 1-55945-223-4

Getting Along With Parents, ISBN 1-55945-202-1

Getting Along With Your Family, ISBN 1-55945-233-1

The Gospel of John: Jesus' Teachings, ISBN 1-55945-208-0

Hazardous to Your Health: AIDS, Steroids & Eating Disorders, ISBN 1-55945-200-5

Is Marriage in Your Future?, ISBN 1-55945-203-X

Jesus' Death & Resurrection, ISBN 1-55945-211-0

The Joy of Serving, ISBN 1-55945-210-2

Knowing God's Will, ISBN 1-55945-205-6

Life After High School, ISBN 1-55945-220-X

Making Good Decisions, ISBN 1-55945-209-9

Money: A Christian Perspective, ISBN 1-55945-212-9

Movies, Music, TV & Me, ISBN 1-55945-213-7

Overcoming Insecurities, ISBN 1-55945-221-8

Psalms, ISBN 1-55945-234-X

Real People, Real Faith: Amy Grant, Joni Eareckson Tada, Dave Dravecky, Terry Anderson, ISBN 1-55945-238-2

Responding to Injustice, ISBN 1-55945-214-5

Revelation, ISBN 1-55945-229-3

School Struggles, ISBN 1-55945-201-3

Sex: A Christian Perspective, ISBN 1-55945-206-4

Today's Lessons From Yesterday's Prophets, ISBN 1-55945-227-7

Turning Depression Upside Down, ISBN 1-55945-135-1

What Is the Church?, ISBN 1-55945-222-6

Who Is God?, ISBN 1-55945-218-8

Who Is Jesus?, ISBN 1-55945-219-6

Who Is the Holy Spirit?, ISBN 1-55945-217-X

Your Life as a Disciple, ISBN 1-55945-204-8

FOR JUNIOR HIGH/MIDDLE SCHOOL:

Accepting Others: Beyond Barriers & Stereotypes, ISBN 1-55945-126-2

Advice to Young Christians: Exploring Paul's Letters, ISBN 1-55945-146-7

Applying the Bible to Life, ISBN 1-55945-116-5

Becoming Responsible, ISBN 1-55945-109-2

Bible Heroes: Joseph, Esther, Mary & Peter, ISBN 1-55945-137-8

Boosting Self-Esteem, ISBN 1-55945-100-9

Building Better Friendships, ISBN 1-55945-138-6

Can Christians Have Fun?, ISBN 1-55945-134-3

Caring for God's Creation, ISBN 1-55945-121-1

Christmas: A Fresh Look, ISBN 1-55945-124-6

Competition, ISBN 1-55945-133-5

Dealing With Death, ISBN 1-55945-112-2

Dealing With Disappointment, ISBN 1-55945-139-4

Doing Your Best, ISBN 1-55945-142-4

Drugs & Drinking, ISBN 1-55945-118-1

Evil and the Occult, ISBN 1-55945-102-5

Genesis: The Beginnings, ISBN 1-55945-111-4

Guys & Girls: Understanding Each Other, ISBN 1-55945-110-6

Handling Conflict, ISBN 1-55945-125-4

Heaven & Hell, ISBN 1-55945-131-9

Is God Unfair?, ISBN 1-55945-108-4

Love or Infatuation?, ISBN 1-55945-128-9

Making Parents Proud, ISBN 1-55945-107-6

Making the Most of School, ISBN 1-55945-113-0

Materialism, ISBN 1-55945-130-0

The Miracle of Easter, ISBN 1-55945-143-2

Miracles!, ISBN 1-55945-117-3

Peace & War, ISBN 1-55945-123-8

Peer Pressure, ISBN 1-55945-103-3

Prayer, ISBN 1-55945-104-1

Reaching Out to a Hurting World, ISBN 1-55945-140-8

Sermon on the Mount, ISBN 1-55945-129-7

Suicide: The Silent Epidemic, ISBN 1-55945-145-9

Telling Your Friends About Christ, ISBN 1-55945-114-9

The Ten Commandments, ISBN 1-55945-127-0

Today's Faith Heroes: Madeline Manning Mims, Michael W. Smith, Mother Teresa, Bruce Olson, ISBN 1-55945-141-6

Today's Media: Choosing Wisely, ISBN 1-55945-144-0

Today's Music: Good or Bad?, ISBN 1-55945-101-7

What Is God's Purpose for Me?, ISBN 1-55945-132-7

What's a Christian?, ISBN 1-55945-105-X

Order today from your local Christian bookstore, or write: Group Publishing, Box 485, Loveland, CO 80539. For mail orders, please add postage/handling of $4 for orders up to $15, $5 for orders of $15.01+. Colorado residents add 3% sales tax.

MORE PROGRAMMING IDEAS FOR YOUR ACTIVE GROUP...

DO IT! ACTIVE LEARNING IN YOUTH MINISTRY

Thom and Joani Schultz

Discover the keys to teaching creative faith-building lessons that teenagers look forward to...and remember for a lifetime. You'll learn how to design simple, fun programs that will help your kids...

- •build community,
- •develop communication skills,
- •relate better to others,
- •experience what it's really like to be a Christian,

...and apply the Bible to their daily challenges. Plus, you'll get 24 ready-to-use active-learning exercises complete with debriefing questions and Bible application. For example, your kids will...

- •learn the importance of teamwork and the value of each team member by juggling six different objects as a group,
- •experience community and God's grace using a doughnut,
- •grow more sensitive to others' needs by acting out Matthew 25:31-46

...just to name a few. And the practical index of over 30 active-learning resources will make your planning easier.

ISBN 0-931529-94-8

DEVOTIONS FOR YOUTH GROUPS ON THE GO

Dan and Cindy Hansen

Now it's easy to turn every youth group trip into an opportunity for spiritual growth for your kids. This resource gives you 52 easy-to-prepare devotions that teach meaningful spiritual lessons using the experiences of your group's favorite outings. You'll get devotions perfect for everything from amusement parks, to choir trips, to miniature golf, to the zoo. Your kids will gain new insights from the Bible as they...

- •discuss how many "strikes" God gives us—after enjoying a game of softball,
- •experience the hardship of Jesus' temptation in the wilderness—on a camping trip,
- •understand the disciples' relief when Jesus calmed the storm—while white-water rafting, even

...learn to trust God's will when bad weather cancels an event or the bus breaks down!

Plus, the handy topical listing makes your planning easy.

ISBN 1-55945-075-4

PUT FAITH INTO ACTION WITH...

Want to try something different with your 7th—12th grade classes? Group's NEW Projects With a Purpose™ for Youth Ministry offers four-week courses that really get kids into their faith. Each Project With a Purpose course gives you tools to facilitate a project that will provide a direct, purposeful learning experience. Teenagers will discover something significant about their faith while learning the importance of working together, sharing one another's troubles, and supporting one another in love...plus they'll have lots of fun!

Each lesson-complete leaders book offers four sessions. Use for Sunday school classes, midweek, home Bible studies, youth groups, retreats, or any time you want to help teenagers discover more about their faith.

These easy-to-teach lessons will help your teenagers learn deep insights about their faith! Your kids will learn more about each other. They'll practice the life skill of working together. And you'll be rewarded with the knowledge that you're providing a life-changing, faith-building experience for your church's teenagers.

Titles Available:

Acting Out Jesus' Parables	1-55945-147-5
Celebrating Christ With Youth-Led Worship	1-55945-410-5
Checking Your Church's Pulse	1-55945-408-3
Serving Your Neighbors	1-55945-406-7
Sharing Your Faith Without Fear	1-55945-409-1
Teaching Teenagers to Pray	1-55945-407-5
Videotaping Your Church Members' Faith Stories	1-55945-239-0